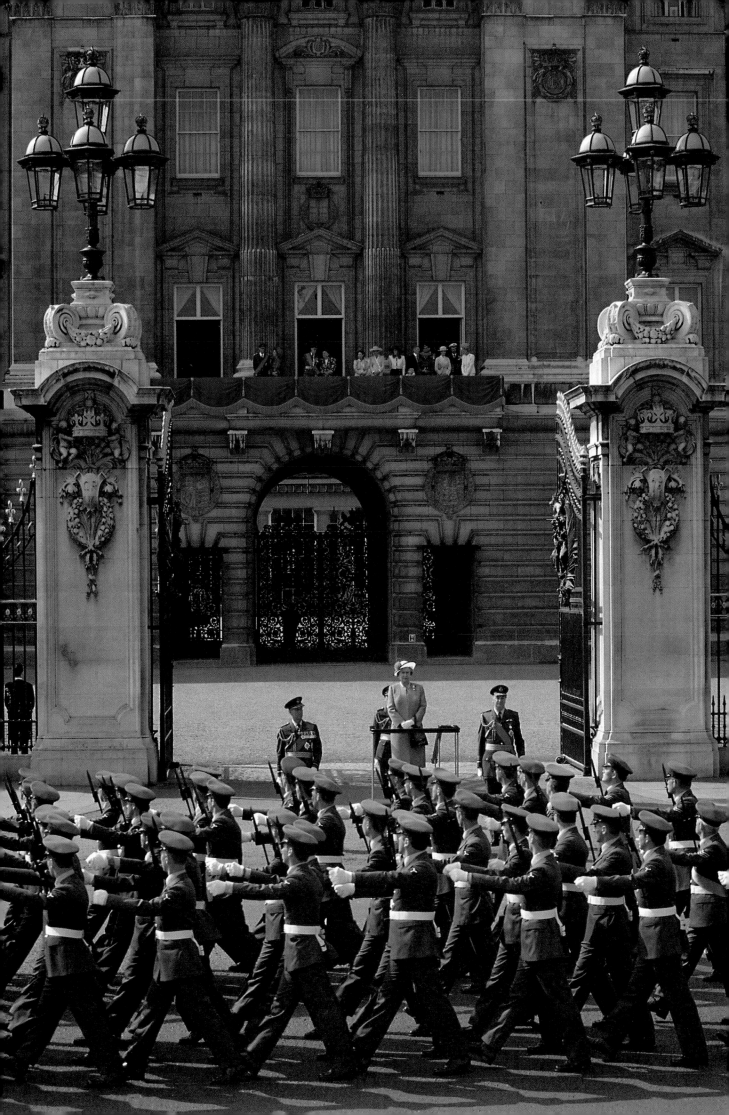

SUMMIT BOOKS
Simon & Schuster Building
Rockefeller Center
1230 Avenue of the Americas
New York, New York 10020

Copyright © 1991 by Tim Graham

Originally published in Great Britain by
Michael O'Mara Books Limited, London

Quality printing and binding in Hong Kong
by Paramount Printing Group Limited

10 9 8 7 6 5 4 3 2 1

Library of Congress cataloging and
publication data available on request

ISBN 0-671-75202-2

THE ROYAL YEAR
1991

PHOTOGRAPHED BY TIM GRAHAM

SUMMIT BOOKS

New York London Toronto Sydney Tokyo

In August the Wales family were again guests of the Spanish royal family at the Marivent Palace on the island of Majorca. Also in the royal party was King Constantine of Greece (whose sister is Queen Sofia) and some of his family. Prince Charles, still recovering from a badly broken arm, had travelled to Majorca in advance of the rest of his family for a few days of peace and quiet staying with friends elsewhere on the island. On board King Juan Carlos's motor cruiser are (below from left to right) King Constantine, Queen Anne-Marie and their youngest daughter Princess Theodora, the Prince and Princess of Wales, King Juan Carlos, Prince William, Queen Sofia, Prince Henry, Infanta Christina and Infanta Elena.

Right: The Princess of Wales, as Patron of the British Deaf Association, attended the charity's centenary congress at Brighton in East Sussex on 9 August, where she revealed her proficiency in sign language.

Below left: The Princess of Wales and Prince William leave Wetherby School on 5 September having dropped off Prince Henry on the first day of term.

Below right and facing page: On 12 September the Duchess of York attended the Amazing Great Children's Party in aid of the Paul O'Gorman Foundation for Children with Leukaemia in Battersea Park, London. Celebrities such as Frank Bruno (below right) attended the party to help give a great day out to over 5000 leukaemic, needy and handicapped children from all over the country.

Left: Princess Beatrice watching the Battle of Britain 50th Anniversary flypast from a window of Buckingham Palace.
Facing page above: The spectacular flypast of nearly 170 Royal Air Force aircraft over Buckingham Palace.

Below: Spectators on the balcony of Buckingham Palace for the Battle of Britain 50th Anniversary celebrations included (from left to right) the Queen, Prince Philip, the King and Queen of the Belgians and Princess Margaret.
Facing page below: The Hon. Sir Angus Ogilvy, the Duchess of Kent, Princess Alexandra and Prince and Princess Michael of Kent on the palace balcony.

Left and page 1: After the fly-past the Queen reviewed a parade of Royal Air Force units and veterans from the forecourt of Buckingham Palace. Many Battle of Britain veterans participated in the parade.

Facing page: The Duchess of York, the Princess of Wales, Prince Henry pointing out something of interest to his cousin Princess Beatrice, and the Duke and Duchess of Kent on the balcony of Buckingham Palace.

Below from left to right: Princess Alexandra, Prince Bernhard and Princess Juliana of the Netherlands, Air Chief Marshal Sir Peter Harding, Prince Henry, the Queen, Prince Philip, the King and Queen of the Belgians, Princess Margaret, the Duchess of York and the Princess of Wales.

Above left: Prince Edward showing his skills at archery at the 'Passport to Adventure' Day at Battersea Park, London, in aid of the Duke of Edinburgh's Award Scheme. Above right: Princess Michael of Kent in striking yellow at a charity ball at the Grosvenor House Hotel, London on 17 September.

Left: The Princess of Wales greeting 91-year-old Nellie Corbett at the John Street Estate in Newham, east London where she spent over 70 minutes talking to residents. Facing page: The Princess of Wales arriving to open the CORE Trust Day Centre in north London on 19 September.

Left: The Duchess of York, Patron of the charity MacIntyre, at a film première in Milton Keynes, Buckinghamshire on 26 September.

Facing page above left: Earlier in the day the Duchess had visited the Milton Keynes General Hospital to open the CT Body Scanner suite and a new outpatients unit.

Above right: The Princess of Wales as Patron of the First International Covent Garden Festival, attended the festival's gala dinner dance at the Garrick Club on 22 September.

Below left: On 28 September Princess Margaret, Grand President of the St John Ambulance Association and Brigade, attended a gala performance at the Chichester Festival Theatre, West Sussex.

Below right: The Princess Royal, as President of the British Knitting and Clothing Export Council, arriving at the Grosvenor House Hotel, London for a trade exhibition.

In early October the Princess of Wales paid a flying visit to Washington of less than 24 hours to carry out a busy programme of engagements. *Far left: Arriving at Dulles International Airport, Washington. Left: At a gala evening in aid of the London City Ballet, the Washington Ballet and Grandma's House, a Washington-based charity for babies and young children suffering from AIDS and drug-related problems. Right: A winning smile from the Princess of Wales between engagements in Washington.*

Below far left: Paying a morning call on Mrs Bush at the White House. Below: On her visit to Grandma's House the Princess befriended a three-year-old resident and (below left) took the little girl for a magical ride in her Rolls Royce around the block to a new Grandma's House, an additional home known affectionately as Grandpa's House which the Princess then opened officially.

Far left: The Duchess of Kent, Patron of the Cancer Relief Macmillan Fund, opened a new hospice care service in Welwyn Garden City, Hertfordshire on 10 October.

Left: The Princess of Wales returned to Towyn in north Wales on 12 October to see the completed sea wall defences, six months after the town suffered from terrible flooding and gales when many people were made homeless.

Right, below left and below right: The Duke and Duchess of York paid a two-day visit to Newcastle in mid-October, including (below right) opening the new Leisure Pool at Prudhoe Waterworld in Northumberland. On the second day of the visit it was the Duchess's birthday and the crowds sang her 'Happy Birthday' wherever she went.

Left: The Princess of Wales arriving at the Sadler's Wells Theatre in a stunning black beaded dress for a gala performance of Ananzi *by the Chicken Shed Theatre company in aid of the Chicken Shed Building Fund.*

Below: At the start of his state visit to Britain on 23 October President Cossiga of Italy was escorted by the Queen from Victoria Station to Buckingham Palace in a carriage procession, the traditional beginning of all state visits to London.
Right: Prince Philip with the President's interpreter during the procession to Buckingham Palace.
On 25 October the President of Italy returned the Queen's hospitality by giving a recital and banquet for the royal family and other distinguished guests at the Victoria and Albert Museum. Seen arriving for the banquet in full evening dress are (far right) the Princess of Wales, the Duchess of Kent (below right) and Princess Margaret (below far right).

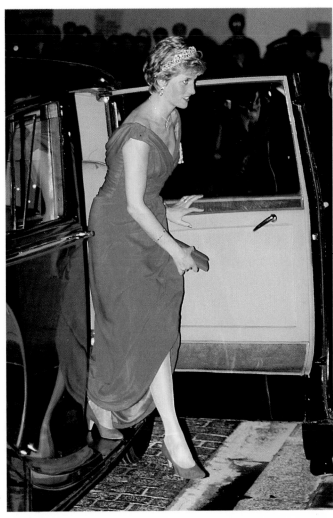

On 25 October during the princes' half-term, the Princess of Wales took Prince William and Prince Henry along with her to a service at St Paul's Cathedral for the veterans of the Fire Brigade during the Blitz 50 years ago. After the service the princes were allowed to inspect two wartime fire engines parked in the cathedral courtyard and Prince Henry much enjoyed pretending to drive a 1937 Leyland Metz tender.

THE DUCHESS OF YORK'S VISIT TO AUSTRALIA

5 – 8 November 1990

In early November the Duchess of York paid a four-day official visit to Australia. The visit was at the invitation of the Royal Flying Doctor Service but the Duchess carried out other engagements in New South Wales and Victoria as well, in particular two engagements concerning the Motor Neurone Disease Society with which she is closely connected.

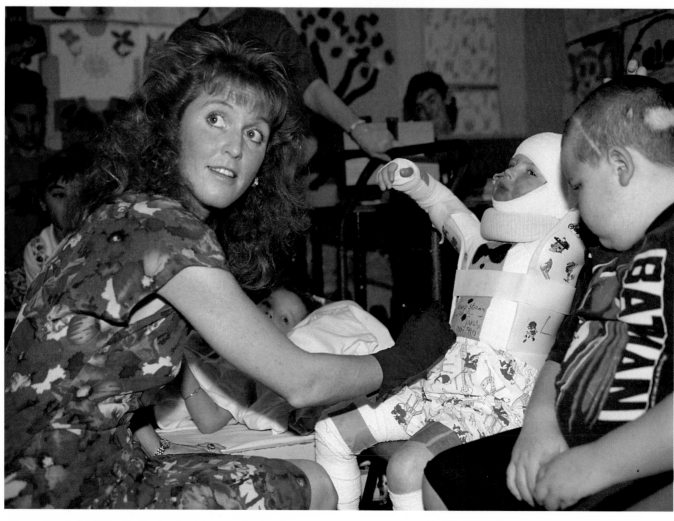

Facing page: On the day of her arrival in Sydney, her second visit to the city, the Duchess of York paid a three-hour visit to the Royal Alexandra Hospital for Children in Camperdown. There she toured the Child Development Unit and met 5-year-old Dean Woodford who was in plaster from head to toe recovering from terrible burns. To cheer him up she wrote a message on his plaster, 'Keep strong. God Bless, Sarah'.

Right: The Duchess arriving at the dinner for the Royal Flying Doctor Service at the Regent Hotel, Sydney when she delivered the third John Flynn Memorial Lecture which keeps alive the tradition of the Service's founder. The biennial lecture is traditionally given by a member of the royal family.

Facing page: The Duchess of York looking stunning in an off-the-shoulder Bellville Sassoon dress for a fund-raising ball in Melbourne. The ball was in aid of the Motor Neurone Disease Society of Victoria and the Duchess gave a speech on the work of Motor Neurone Societies in Britain. Right: At the School of Air in Broken Hill, a mining town in the Australian outback, the Duchess of York spoke on the radio to various pupils, some of them many hundreds of miles away. Below left: At the Barrier Pre-School for Disabled Children in Broken Hill. Below right: Arriving at the Westmead Neurological Society in Sydney where the Duchess met patients suffering from Motor Neurone Disease.

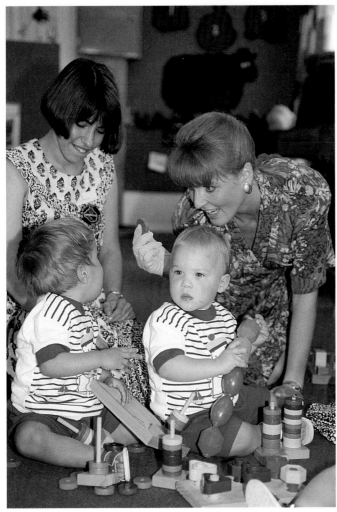

THE PRINCE AND PRINCESS OF WALES IN JAPAN

10 – 14 November 1990

The Prince and Princess of Wales travelled to Japan in November where the Prince represented the Queen at the enthronement ceremony of Emperor Akihito of Japan, the first enthronement of a new emperor since 1928. For the first time outside guests and television cameras were allowed to view the ceremony, full of ancient ritual and splendid costumes. Distinguished visitors from all over the world came to Tokyo for the occasion.

Facing page above: The Prince and Princess of Wales at the enthronement ceremony. The Princess's eyecatching silk headband and veil were an instant winner. Facing page below: At a Remembrance Day Service at the Commonwealth War Graves Cemetery in Hodogaya. Above: The Princess of Wales talking to children at the National Children's Hospital in Tokyo. Right: The Princess of Wales greeting Prince Hendrik of Denmark at the imperial garden party given by the Emperor and Empress. The Princess of Wales delighted her Japanese hosts by decorating her pillbox hat with the Japanese emblem of a rising sun.

Left: The Princess of Wales wearing protective glasses during a visit to a Honda car factory in Tokyo on 14 November. Below and facing page: That evening the Prince and Princess of Wales attended a performance of Salome *by the Welsh National Opera in Tokyo.*

Left: The Princess of Wales visited Oxford on 20 November to carry out five official engagements. Below: Talking to crowds outside the University College Hospital's Drug Dependence Clinic in central London. Facing page left: Arriving in glittering sequins and emeralds for the Diamond Ball at the Royal Lancaster Hotel, in aid of the charity, Schizophrenia. Above right: The Duchess of York at the Middlesex Hospital to open Britain's first Teenage Cancer Unit. Below right: The Princess of Wales in bright yellow satin for a gala evening at the London Palladium in aid of the Prince's Trust.

The Princess of Wales paid a one-day visit to Brussels on 10 December to carry out various engagements. Facing page: It was British Week at the INNO department store and the Princess of Wales came to see the display of British goods on sale. Above: Talking to patients and staff at the Queen Fabiola Children's Hospital. Right: Travelling around Brussels in the rain.

Left: On 14 December the Princess of Wales reviewed the Sovereign's Parade at the Royal Military Academy, Sandhurst and took the salute on behalf of the Queen. In her speech at the ceremony she sent warm words of encouragement to the servicemen out in the Gulf.

On 21 December the Queen and Prince Philip visited RAF Benson to accept a new jet for the Queen's Flight. Below left: Talking to airmen at the base. Right: Receiving a specially commissioned silver model of the new aircraft. Below: The traditional group photograph with the staff of the Queen's Flight.

The christening of nine-month-old Princess Eugenie Victoria Helena of York took place on 23 December at the parish church at Sandringham after the Sunday morning service. Left: After the christening there was a cuddle from the Duchess of York for Princess Eugenie who had cried during much of the service. Below: The Duke and Duchess of York with Princess Eugenie. Facing page above: Leaving church after the service, the Duke and Duchess of York with Princess Eugenie, Zara Phillips and the Queen. Facing page below: Members of the royal family at the church gate with godparents and the Bishop of Norwich who had performed the christening ceremony.

In January the Duchess of York took Princess Beatrice for a short winter holiday to teach her daughter her own favourite winter sport. This was the second year running that two-and-a-half-year-old Princess Beatrice had visited Klosters with the Duchess. Left: Arriving in Zurich wearing similar brown leather jackets. Below and facing page: Princess Beatrice being helped to stand on tiny skis.

The Princess of Wales travelled to the military base of Sennelage in Germany on 31 January to pay a morale-boosting visit to families of servicemen on duty in the Gulf. The Princess admitted during the visit she had been glued to television coverage of the conflict, then in its second week.

During the Gulf conflict the royal family paid numerous visits to military units both in Britain and overseas. On 11 February the Prince and Princess of Wales paid a joint visit to HM Naval Base at Devonport. Right: For the visit Prince Charles wore the uniform of a Royal Navy captain. Below: The Princess of Wales joking with workers at the naval dockyard.

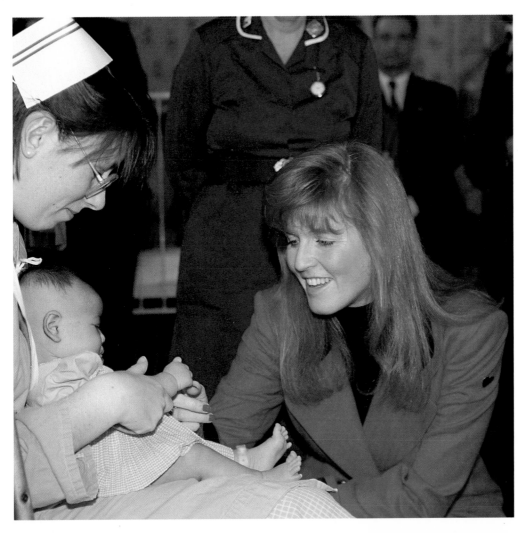

Left and below left: The Duchess of York visited the Derbyshire Children's Hospital on 14 February.
Below right: The Princess of Wales, as President of the Royal Marsden Hospital, attended a banquet at the Guildhall, London in aid of Britain's leading cancer hospital on 18 February. The six-course dinner was prepared by some of Britain's foremost chefs.

Left: The Princess of Wales took Prince Henry to the Royal Albert Hall on 20 February for the 1991 Mountbatten Festival of Music.

Right: The Queen and Prince Philip visited Port Regis School in Dorset on 22 February to open the Queen's Hall, the school's new gymnastics centre. The Queen and Prince Philip's oldest grandchildren, Peter and Zara Phillips are pupils at the school. Below: Zara Phillips during the gymnastics display put on for the royal visitors. Facing page above: Peter Phillips showing the Queen a burglar alarm system he had designed. Facing page below: The Queen and Prince Philip being escorted to lunch by their grandchildren.

Left: The Princess Royal was in Windsor on 27 February to attend the Circle of Friendship Annual Blanket Thanksgiving Service and to receive blankets made for Save the Children Fund, of which she is President. Below left: Prince Philip visited the London Docklands to open the Innovation Centre, which offers facilities to small pioneering companies.

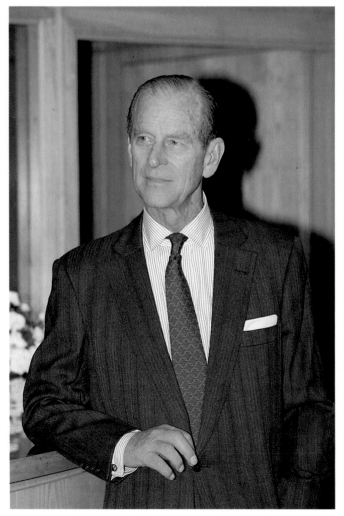

Right, below left and below: On 1 March, St David's Day (the patron saint of Wales), the Prince and Princess of Wales took Prince William with them for the St David's Day Service at Llandaff Cathedral, Cardiff. It was Prince William's first visit to Wales and he marked the occasion by wearing the Welsh traditional daffodil in the lapel of his blazer, while his parents both sported the symbol of the leek, the national emblem of Wales. Local schoolchildren lined the route to the cathedral and cheered Prince William as he passed by.

Left: The Princess of Wales, Patron of the British Lung Foundation, visited the British Telecom Headquarters in London on 13 March, No Smoking Day, to hear at first hand about the aims and achievements of the campaign.
Right: The Duchess of York with Princess Beatrice, one of the bridesmaids, at the wedding of the Duchess's close friend, Lulu Blacker.

Facing page and below: The Princess of Wales accompanied the Prince of Wales to Manchester on 12 March to carry out a number of engagements. On walkabout outside the Manchester City Art Gallery she received an enthusiastic welcome from the crowds.

Right and facing page left: The Princess of Wales travelled to RAF Scampton, Lincolnshire on 14 March to meet families of both British and American servicemen and women serving in the Gulf and talked to the crowds during her walkabout on the airfield.

Below: As President, the Princess of Wales visited the Great Ormond Street Hospital for Children on 18 March.

Below: Princess Michael of Kent at the London Palladium for a gala performance of Showboat *in aid of the Royal London Society for the Blind and the Park Lane Group.*

Facing page left and far left: The Duchess of York in Winchester on 19 March, showing off a dashing new hairstyle for the first time in public, at a service of celebration for the 5th anniversary of Age Concern Hampshire and the 50th anniversary of Age Concern England, of which she is Patron.

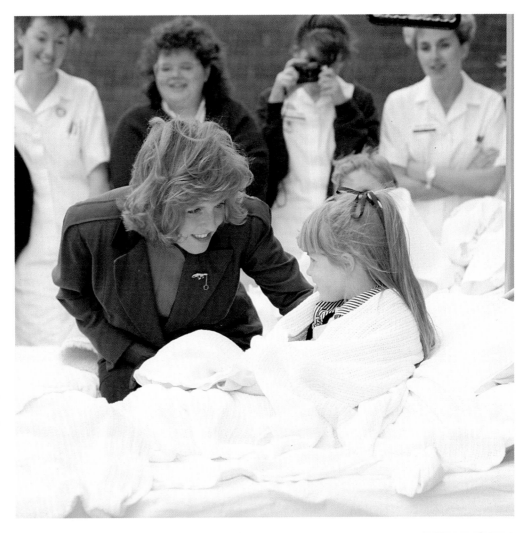

Right, below left and below right: The following day, 20 March, the Duchess of York, Countess of Inverness, flew to Inverness in northern Scotland to carry out a full day of engagements, including visiting the Disabled Living and Wheelchair Centre at the Raigmore Hospital.

The memorial service for King Olav of Norway, one of Europe's most popular monarchs who died aged 87 on 17 January, took place in Westminster Abbey on 21 March and was attended by many members of the royal family including the Queen (above), Princess Margaret (above right) and the Queen Mother (right) who was a very old friend of the King's. Born at Sandringham, the royal estate in Norfolk, King Olav was a grandson of Edward VII and therefore closely related to the British royal family.

Right: A cheeky smile from Prince Henry as he left St George's Chapel after the traditional Easter Day Service at Windsor Castle.

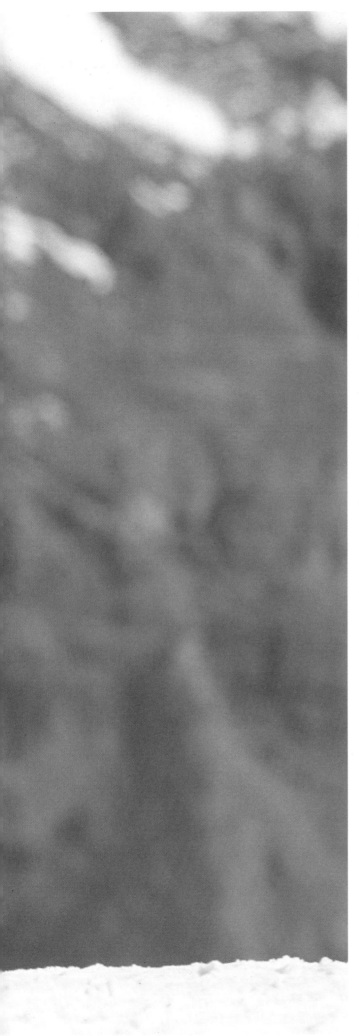

Left and below: After Easter the Princess of Wales took the two princes on their first skiing holiday to the picturesqe resort of Lech in Austria. Overleaf: Soaring up the mountainside on a chairlift was an exhilarating experience for the princes who had spent the first few days of the holiday lower down on the nursery slopes.

Above and right: Learning to ski is not always as easy as it looks, even for young princes, as Prince Henry found out on the first day of their skiing holiday.

*Right: Prince William learning the art of snowploughing.
Below: Prince Henry keeping up with the Princess of Wales and the instructor on the piste high up on the mountain.*

THE PRINCE AND PRINCESS OF WALES IN BRAZIL

22 – 27 April 1991

The visit by the Prince and Princess of Wales to Brazil was originally scheduled for the autumn of 1990 but was then postponed due to Prince Charles's broken arm. The Prince had visited Brazil in 1978 and this time he was keen that the tour should concentrate on environmental issues, as well as including visits to the major Brazilian cities.

Facing page: On the first day of the tour the Prince and Princess of Wales travelled to Carajas, a mining region deep in the Amazon jungle, where they inspected a vast open cast mine and then planted a nut tree as a symbolic gesture to help the reforestation programme under way.
This page: While at Carajas the Princess of Wales showed her magic touch with children. During her visit to a local school she was immediately befriended by the children, two of whom stayed glued to her side throughout her stay.

For the official dinner given by the President of Brazil in the capital, Brasilia, the Princess of Wales wore a stunning pink and white embroidered evening dress with the spectacular Queen Mary pearl and diamond tiara, given to her as a wedding present by the Queen.

On the same day as her departure for Brazil the Princess, as Patron of the National Aids Trust, had opened a conference in London with a speech calling on people to reach out and help victims of the HIV virus. In São Paulo the Princess of Wales showed that she practises what she preaches and paid a moving visit to the Foundation for Welfare of Minors hostel for abandoned children, many of them physically or mentally handicapped or HIV-positive. The children flocked around her and begged to be held and hugged by the beautiful lady who had come to visit them. The Princess was much moved by the plight of these tragic children who are starved of affection.

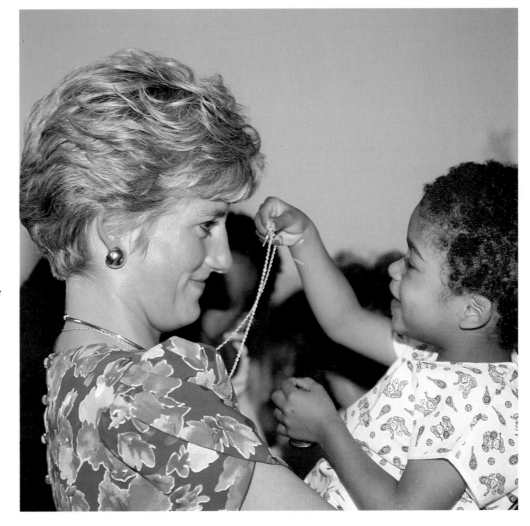

On the third day of the tour the Prince and Princess of Wales were in Rio de Janeiro. While Prince Charles concentrated on visits to manufacturing and industrial sites near Rio, the Princess carried out several engagements in the city. Right: Watching a dancing display at a street children's refuge. Below: Talking to a patient in the Aids ward at the University Hospital.

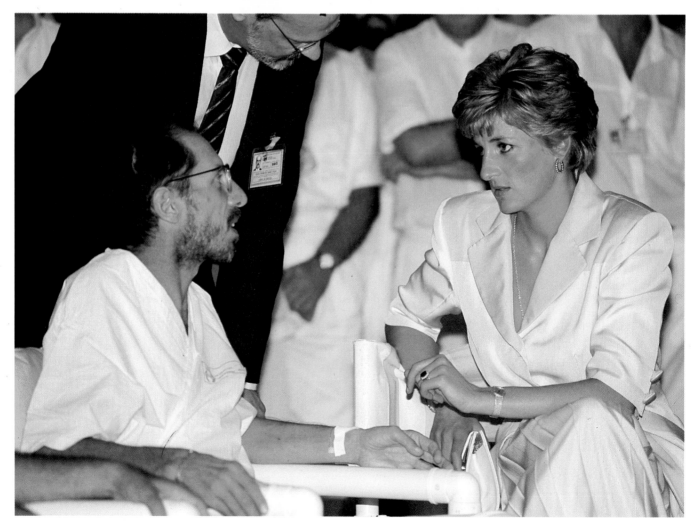

Above: Late afternoon in Rio was reserved for a spot of sightseeing. Rio de Janeiro has a magnificent location, sandwiched between the mountains and the Atlantic Ocean, and to get a panoramic view of the city and the famous Sugarloaf Mountain the Princess took a cable-car to the top of Corcovado Mountain, the symbol of Rio, and then climbed to the viewing platform right at the top. Right: For the dinner given in their honour by the State Governor and Mayor of Rio the Princess of Wales wore a bright pink lace dress.

Left: While the Prince of Wales was co-hosting an environmental seminar on board HMY Britannia at Belem, the Princess travelled south to the Argentine border to Foz do Iguaçu to marvel at the spectacular Cataratas waterfalls, the largest in the world. Below: For a charity gala ballet performance at the Municipal Theatre on the last evening in Rio the Princess wore a stunning off-the-shoulder white dress.

Above left and right: While touring the 5th International Contemporary Art Fair in London in April the Duchess of York met Lady Helen Windsor who was manning a stand at the fair.

Facing page below and this page: On 2 May the Duchess of York, as patron of MacIntyre, visited the charity's project in Aylesbury, Buckinghamshire, which helps school-leavers with mental disabilities make the transition to adult life in the community.

THE PRINCE AND PRINCESS OF WALES VISIT CZECHOSLOVAKIA

6 – 9 May 1991

The Prince and Princess of Wales's visit to Czechoslovakia was their second trip to Eastern Europe, having been invited to Hungary in the summer of 1990. President Havel of Czechoslovakia had invited the royal couple to make an official visit to put a seal of approval on the country's new democracy and transition to a free market.

Facing page below: Prince
Charles and President Havel at
the welcoming ceremony in front
of Prague Castle. Facing page
above: The Prince and Princess
of Wales pausing in front of the
memorial commemorating victims of 40 years of communist
repression in Wenceslas Square,
the heart of medieval Prague.

Above: Vast crowds gave an
emotional welcome to the royal
couple during their visit to
Wenceslas Square. Left: The
Princess of Wales meeting a
pupil at the Zakladni School
for Hard of Hearing Children
in Prague.

Facing page far left: On a chilly visit to Devín Castle, overlooking the River Danube near Bratislava, a gallant Czech offered the Princess of Wales his coat to keep her warm. Facing page left and above left: To commemorate the bicentenary of Mozart's death in 1791 the Princess of Wales visited the Bertramka Mozart Museum in Prague where the composer had lived for a while. Above right and right: For her last engagement in Czechoslovakia the Princess of Wales accompanied Prince Charles and President and Mrs Havel to the Commonwealth War Graves Cemetery for a wreath-laying ceremony during which they met Czech World War II veterans. The Princess of Wales then returned to London while Prince Charles stayed on for further enagagements.

At this year's Royal Windsor Horse Show in the middle of May the young Princess Beatrice stole the show. Facing page: Enjoying a ride on her mother's shoulders. Above left: Princess Beatrice modelling the shocking pink butterfly sunglasses bought for her at the show fairground by the Duchess of York. Above right: The Queen in a relaxed mood while presenting prizes at the Horse Show. Right: Princess Eugenie enjoyed every moment of eating her ice cream.

14 – 17 May 1991

In May the Queen paid her first state visit to Washington DC since 1976. The aim of the visit was that it should be a 'meet-the-people' tour and the Queen's busy schedule included eighteen engagements in four days. After Washington the Queen and Prince Philip set off to visit Florida and Texas.

Facing page: The first morning of the state visit was taken up with a colourful arrival ceremony on the White House lawn which included music played by American soldiers dressed as revolutionary fife-and-drummers in traditional ceremonial uniform. Right: Prince Philip and Mrs Bush listening to the speeches made by the Queen and President Bush during the ceremony. Below left: President Bush demonstrated to the Queen the art of throwing horseshoes, a traditional American backyard game, and she presented him with a set of horseshoes engraved with her cypher. Below right: For the arrival ceremony the Queen wore regal purple with a striking purple and white boater to match her suit.

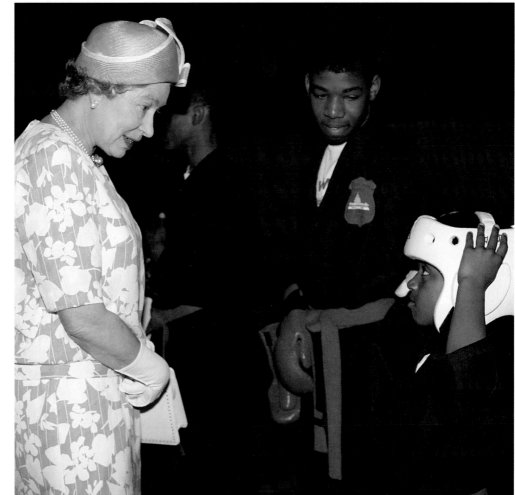

Facing page above: The Queen and Prince Philip with President and Mrs Bush before the state dinner given in the royal couple's honour at the White House. Facing page below: The Queen and Mrs Bush visiting the Richard England Clubhouse where they watched a display of martial arts and gymnastics put on by local children. Right: The Queen meeting a young boxer at the Clubhouse. Below left and right: On the third day of the visit the Queen and Prince Philip paid a visit to the Capitol where the Queen addressed a Joint Meeting of the US Congress, the first time that a British monarch had done so. Her speech was enthusiastically received and was interrupted six times by applause.

Facing page above: After lunch at the Capitol the royal party moved on to visit Mount Vernon, the home of George Washington, the first president of the USA, which lies just outside the city. The elegant home is surrounded by beautiful gardens and woodland which the Queen was able to admire briefly.
Facing page below: The Queen and Prince Philip were hosts at a garden party held at the British Embassy for prominent Americans, mainly from the Washington area. Seen here with the Queen and Prince Philip are the Vice-President and Mrs Quayle.

Above and left: The last engagement in Washington was a short service at the recently completed Washington National Cathedral.

Facing page: The Queen, an enthusiastic follower of flat racing, rarely misses Derby Day at Epsom Races. This year's Derby Day took place on 5 June, and included in the royal party were (above left) the Queen, (above right) the Queen Mother, (below left) Prince Philip, who celebrated his 70th birthday the following week, and (below right) the Duchess of Gloucester.

Left: The Princess of Wales arriving for a gala organ recital at St Martin-in-the-Fields Church in central London. Below left: On 10 June the Prince and Princess of Wales visited Münster in Germany for the Drumhead Service of Remembrance and Thanksgiving in honour of Army and RAF units who served in the Gulf War. The Princess of Wales is seen here chatting to servicemen before the victory lunch. Below right: On 12 June the Duchess of York went to the Royal County of Berkshire Polo Club for an afternoon of polo.

Right: The Princess of Wales enjoying an informal afternoon at Wetherby School Sports Day in Richmond, south-west London. Facing page above: Prince Henry (centre) taking part in the sack race. Below left: Running barefoot, the Princess of Wales (second left) taking part in a hard fought mothers' race. Below: The Princess of Wales talking to children at a crèche at Treforest in Mid-Glamorgan, Wales.

Facing page above: The Queen leaving Buckingham Palace on her way to Horse Guards Parade for Trooping the Colour, the ceremonial review held each year in June to mark the sovereign's official birthday. Following on horseback are the Prince of Wales, Prince Philip, the Duke of Kent and the Grand Duke of Luxembourg. Below left: The Queen Mother was accompanied by the Princess of Wales and Prince Henry as she drove to Horse Guards Parade to watch the ceremony. Prince William did not take part as he was recovering from an operation. This page: After returning from Horse Guards Parade the Queen stood in the Centre Gateway of Buckingham Palace to review the Guards as they marched past and then joined other members of the royal family and guests on the palace balcony to watch the traditional flypast up The Mall by the Royal Air Force.

The annual Garter Day Ceremony takes place in the middle of June at Windsor Castle. The Most Noble Order of the Garter is the oldest order of chivalry in Britain, dating from the mid-fourteenth century. The Queen (facing page) is head of the Order and joins the colourful procession of Knights from Windsor Castle to St George's Chapel for the Garter Day Service. Above: The Queen Mother, a Lady of the Garter, walking in procession with the Knights, including (left) the King of the Belgians who was installed as an Extra Knight Companion at this year's ceremony. Left: The Princess of Wales accompanied the Queen of the Belgians in the Garter carriage procession.

The four-day Royal Ascot Meeting, with its excellent flat racing and elegant fashions, is one of the highlights of the English summer season. Intermittent showers on the first day did not, however, prevent the royal family's traditional carriage procession down the course to the Royal Enclosure before the start of the afternoon's racing. *Left:* The Queen and Prince Philip head the procession of open landaus. *Below far left:* The Princess of Wales wore a striking white suit with black accessories and carried an umbrella to fend off the rain. *Below left and below:* The Princess of Wales and the Duchess of York both wore eye-catching hats on the second day of the Royal Meeting. *Right:* The Queen Mother and the Princess of Wales drive down the course on the second day.

Overleaf: At the Gulf War Welcome Home Parade organized by the City of London at the Mansion House on 21 June, the Queen reviewed the marchpast of serving men and women who had all participated in the war.